The Kingdom Prophet...
...who is the Kingdom Intercessor

The True Identity of

The KINGDOM PROPHET...
...is The KINGDOM INTERCESSOR

BY PERNELL H. HEWING, PH.D., TH.D.

Copyright © 2013 by Pernell H. Hewing
All Rights Reserved

THE KINGDOM PROPHET...
...WHO IS THE INTERCESSOR

SANCTUARY WORD PRESS
Pernell H. Hewing, Ph.D., Th.D.
921 W. Main Street
Whitewater, Wisconsin 53190
(262) 473-7472 -- Fax: (262) 473-9724
E-Mail: hewingph@idcnet.com
Web Page: www.sanctuarywhitewater.com

This publication is a tool to teach, train, and inform Christians. Also **Sanctuary Word Press** will minister and lead Christians into a deep ministry of God's word and God's work.

All rights reserved. No part of this publication may be reproduced or transmitted in any form or by any means—electronic or mechanical—including photo-copy recording or any information storage and retrieval system, without permission in writing from the publisher.

Some scripture quotations are from the King James Bible (C) 1908, 1917, 1929, 1934, 1957, 1964, 1982 by the B.B. Kirkridge Bible Co., Inc.

For additional information about **Sanctuary Word Press,** call **(262) 473-7472.**

Printed in the United States of America
Copyright 2013 by Pernell H. Hewing

The Kingdom Prophet...
...who is the Kingdom Intercessor

The True Identity of

The KINGDOM INTERCESSOR...
...is The KINGDOM PROPHET

BY PERNELL H. HEWING, PH.D., TH.D.

The *Kingdom prophet who is the intercessor*

"Wherefore take unto you the whole armour of God, that ye may be able to withstand in the evil day, and having done all, to stand.

"Stand therefore, having your loins girt about with truth, and having on the breastplate of righteousness;

"And your feet shod with the preparation of the gospel of peace;

"Above all, taking the shield of faith, wherewith ye shall be able to quench all the fiery darts of the wicked.

"And take the helmet of salvation, and the sword of the Spirit, which is the word of God:

"Praying always with all prayer and supplication in the Spirit, and watching thereunto with all perseverance and supplication for all saints;"
Ephesians 6:13-18

Preface

The fullness of time has come for the true identity of the Kingdom prophet to be revealed--an identity which is inextricably interwoven into the identity of intercessor. When God calls one whom He can trust to be His Kingdom prophet, woven into that call is the call to be a Kingdom intercessor. As the prophet or prophetess lives, moves and has his/her being in prayer and intercession, he/she stands as that watchman, and as that intercessor, and as that guide to prepare God's end-time Church for the return of Jesus Christ.

The Lord issues this call to the one prepared to be His completely and His only. The Lord wants to trust a 'called-out' one to prepare His church for the close of the age and the return of Christ. If that one is not His completely, the King cannot trust that one to follow Him wholeheartedly. For that reason the training has been intense for the prophet and for the intercessor over the past years.

The present-day Prophetic Movement ushers in the end-time battle of the Age. This is a battle which must be fought in the heavenly as well as in the Church; therefore, there must be and has been training on every front in preparation for the Kingdom Church to come forth. For that reason, intercession has been on the forefront of training in the midst of the training that is ongoing for the prophet.

For new church awakening, the prophets are out front, and are the intercessors on the frontline with them or are the prophets the intercessors? The fullness of time has come for the prophets and the intercessors to understand that etched in the call as prophet of the King and for the Kingdom is the call to be a *Kingdom prophet who is the intercessor*.

It is not the purpose of this book to add nor take away from what is already written about the prophetic ministry. It is not a book to elaborate on what has been written about intercession nor to criticize what is happening with the prophetic or intercession. The purpose of this writing is to present a Kingdom prospective on the identity of the Kingdom Prophet as Kingdom intercessor preparing for the awakening of the church.

Some reading this may know much more about this topic than this writer. However, having written more than 65 books on intercession, many of which provide fundamental truth about the prophet who is the intercessor, this writer believes that the fullness of time has come to reveal how inextricably interwoven the ministry of the prophetic and intercession are.

It is hoped that this book will present a new prospective on who is the Kingdom prophet and who is the Kingdom intercessor. Is the Kingdom prophet and Kingdom intercessor the same person? My plea, dear reader, is that you read this book before assuming anything because it may add to what you already know, but many who are prophets have not understood that the call to the office of the prophet is undergirded with strategic preparation for intercession.

All the prophets of the Old Testament were intercessors, and New Testament Kingdom prophets will of necessity be established firmly as intercessors for the Kingdom church. It is a fact that Old Testament prophets were called by God to walk and minister in the Office of a prophet. Therefore, one can assume that they, too, had been prepared by doing something God noted that made them fit to be called to the office of the prophet.

As the church has been preparing for its Kingdom position, prophets and intercessors have been spawned across the landscape of the church—mostly giving personal prophecy and sometimes a word for the Church Body. Many of them have proven that they are prophets and they are also intercessors. It could be that these current church prophets are the ones God is going to call to the office of Kingdom prophet intercessor. It may be that God will raise up a new breed and train them to be His **Kingdom prophet who is the intercessor.**

Finally, there are many burgeoning prophets who have a call from the Lord to be His Kingdom prophet. These blessed ones have been in training for some time and have been serving as prophets, but have they taken on the mantle of intercession that accompanies the call to the office of the prophet? Is there a need for the established prophets to train the burgeoning prophets and prepare them for intercession? May this book open the way for this all-important Kingdom move of the merging of Kingdom prophetic and Kingdom intercession.

Pernell H. Hewing, Author

The call for the *Kingdom prophet who is the intercessor* to come Forth for...

It is written...

> "Again he said unto me, Prophesy upon these bones, and say unto them, O ye dry bones, hear the word of the Lord." Ezekiel 37:4

> "So I prophesied as I was commanded: and as I prophesied, there was a noise, and behold a shaking, and the bones came together, bone to his bone.

> "And when I beheld, lo, the sinews and the flesh came upon them and the skin covered them above: but there was no breath in them.

> "Then said he unto me, Prophesy unto the wind, prophesy, son of man, and say to the wind, Thus saith the Lord God; Come from the four winds, O breath and breathe upon these slain, that they may live."
> Ezekiel 37:7-9

Table of Contents

Preface 5

PART I. The Kingdom Prophet who is the Intercessor 11

Chapter 1

    The call of the Prophet Who is the Intercessor. 13

Chapter 2

    The Kingdom Prophet Intercessor Carries two Burdens for the Church 23

Chapter 3

    The Making of a Kingdom Prophet who is the Intercessor 33

Chapter 4

    The Office of the Kingdom Prophet Requires Death to Self 39

PART II: THE WORK OF THE KINGDOM PROPHET WHO IS THE INTERCESSOR..........................53

Chapter 5

    Intercession Brings Understanding of the Prophetic Assignment......................................55

Chapter 6

    The Role of the Hidden Ones 59

Chapter 7

    The Kingdom Prophet is a Kingdom Intercessor 67

Chapter 8

    The Call is Personal. Who will Answer? 75

Books by Pernell H. Hewing 89

PART I

The Call of the...
Prophet...
...who is THE
...Intercessor

"Also I heard the voice of the Lord, saying, Whom shall I send, and who will go for us? Then said I, Here I am; send me." Isaiah 6:8

The Kingdom Prophet...
Called to be...
.....The Intercessor

"Then said I, Woe is me! For I am undone; because I am a man of unclean lips, and I dwell in the midst of a people of unclean lips; for mine eyes have seen the King, the LORD of hosts." Isaiah 6:5

The Preparation...

"Then flew one of the seraphims unto me, having a live coal in his hand, which he had taken with the tongs from off the altar.

"And he laid it upon my mouth, and said, Lo, this hath touched thy lips; and thine iniquity is taken away, and thy sin purged." Isaiah 6:6-7

Chapter 1

THE CALL TO THE OFFICE OF THE PROPHET WHO IS THE INTERCESSOR

"And take the helmet of salvation, and the sword of the Spirit, which is the word of God:

"Praying always with all prayer and supplication in the Spirit, and watching thereunto with all perseverance and supplication for all saints," Ephesians 6:17-18

As one touches the throne of God in this period of Church History, one may be awestruck as the curtain is pulled back in the Spirit, and one sees what is happening in the spiritual realm and what time it is on God's time clock. One will note that much of what has been released in the Church has been a preparation for where the Church is today as it struggles to arise.

The Lord loves His Church and is seeking ones He can trust to co-labor with Him to do an important work. It is written...

> "That he might sanctify and cleanse it with the washing of water by the word,
>
> "That he might present it to himself a glorious church, not having spot, or wrinkle, or any such thing; but that it should be holy and without blemish." Ephesians 5:26-27

The prophetic ministry and the intercessory prayer ministry have certainly had a leading role in this End-of-Age preparation. In recent years, every end-time ministry of the church was interwoven into the prophetic ministry and the intercessory prayer ministry although the Church too often considered them as separate ministries. With that mindset, the ministry of inter-cession and the ministry of the prophet have not been accurately identified.

The call of a Kingdom prophet is more than the call of the prophet who gives personal prophesies, and the Kingdom call of the Kingdom intercessor is more than the call of one who prays and/or wars. The **Kingdom prophet** is an intercessor, a prophet, a prophetic intercessor, a watchman, a spiritual father or mother, a pastor, a shepherd of the flock and a prayer warrior.

God is calling forth Kingdom prophets to be God's mouth to the Church in Preparation for The End-Time Battle of the Age to open the way for the Kingdom to come on earth as it is in heaven. It is written...

> *"And as they departed, Jesus began to say ... concerning John, What went ye out into the wilderness to see? A reed shaken with the wind?*
>
> *"But what went ye out for to see? A man clothed in soft raiment? behold, they that wear soft clothing are in kings' houses.*
>
> *"But what went ye out for to see? A prophet? yea, I say unto you, and more than a prophet.*

"For this is he, of whom it is written, Behold, I send my messenger before thy face, which shall prepare thy way before thee.

"Verily I say unto you, Among them that are born of women there hath not risen a greater than John the Baptist: notwithstanding he that is least in the kingdom of heaven is greater than he."
Matthew 11:7-11

The present-day Prophetic Movement ushers in the end-time battle of the Age. Every believer lives, moves, and ministers in the midst of a prophetic movement of God. The people of God are the prophetic people of **God's** prophetic movement, and the New Testament Kingdom Church is the hub of this strategic movement.

It is imperative, therefore, that the **New Testament Kingdom Church** understands God's Prophetic movement. For the Church to awaken to its Kingdom Call, Church leaders needs must understand how God's present Prophetic Movement is inextricably interwoven into God's eternal purpose and co-labor with God in the present Prophetic Movement.

The **New Testament Kingdom Church** must understand God's present-day Prophetic Movement, how it fits into God's eternal purpose, and how the **New Testament, End-Time** *Believer/Saint's* eternal purpose is tied into **God's Prophetic Movement** and God's eternal purpose. One will then understand the call to and the understanding of the ministry of one's call to the **Office of the Prophet** and how one is established as a prophet who is the intercessor.

The Holy Bible is a treatise of God's Prophetic Movements. Paul caught a glimpse of God's Prophetic Movement ushered in by Jesus Christ for the Church. Paul was in the forefront of a new prophetic movement, and His writing suggests His call to intercession for the prophetic people to which he was called. It is written...

> *"Unto me, who am less than the least of all saints, is this grace given, that I should preach among the Gentiles the unsearchable riches of Christ;*
>
> *"And to make all men see what is the fellowship of the mystery, which from the beginning of the world hath been hid in God, who created all things by Jesus Christ:*
>
> *"To the intent that now unto the principalities and powers in heavenly places might be known by the church the manifold wisdom of God,*
>
> *"According to the eternal purpose which he purposed in Christ Jesus our Lord:*
>
> *"In whom we have boldness and access with confidence by the faith of him."* Ephesians 3:8-12

NEW TESTAMENT *BELIEVERS* ARE GOD'S PROPHETIC PEOPLE

A Prophetic Movement is God's dispensation the purpose of which is to restore what needs restoring to fulfill God's eternal purpose. Significant ones in God's prophetic movement are the prophet and the prophetic people. Also important to a prophetic movement is a plan for restoration of that which was lost that prevents God's eternal purpose from being fulfilled. The New Testament

Kingdom prophetic movement is God's strategic plan and work to restore all things necessary to bring in His New Testament Kingdom Church into God's eternal purpose for the Church.

> Get Ready: The Lord is calling forth
> *His Prepared Prophets who are Intercessors*
> for the Office of
> Kingdom Prophet Intercessor
>
> *"...unto you that fear my name shall the Sun of righteousness arise with healing in his wings;..."*
> Malachi 4:2-3

The design of a **Prophetic Movement** is orchestrated by the Holy Spirit to carry out God's plan and to work to restore truth of God which was lost to the Church. The Lord is bringing forth Kingdom prophetic ministries today because the Lord knows that the office of the prophet is key to restoration of truths to the church to win the Battle of the Age and to open the way for the Kingdom to come on earth as it is in heaven.

Because God's Prophetic Movements are led by God's prophetic people in a prophetic ministry, the New Testament Kingdom Church needs to believe in and understand fully the dimension of the prophetic ministry for the New Testament Kingdom Church.

The purpose of the initial prophetic ministry preparation was established for the prophetic Apostles, watchmen, prayer warriors, intercessors, spiritual fathers/mothers, shepherds of the flock, worshippers, and teachers. During the years, many answered the call to these various ministries, however, some may not have grasped the Kingdom purpose of the prophetic.

The above special ministries of the Church have often been isolated as a special calling and rightly so, but the purposes of each dictates that they not be seen or entered into in isolation. When the prophetic ministry was released to the Church, the purpose was not to end with personal prophecy to God's people, but to prepare God's people to hear the voice of God and to understand God's mind for His prophetic people.

The time has come now for each of the different ministries of the church to enter into its prophetic purpose with prophetic intercession as the main function of that particular ministry. It is important, therefore, for the mind of five-fold ministers and saints to be expanded to include the title of prophetic intercessor in front of the title of the apostle, prophet, pastor, worshipper, spiritual father mother, teacher, etc. This also includes apostolic intercessor, prophetic watchman intercessor and prophetic prayer warrior.

To prepare the church and its prophetic people for ascent into the Kingdom, these ministers will have to acknowledge the prophetic and intercessory purpose of their call. The prophet intercessor brings the Kingdom, prophetic ministry and Kingdom intercession to the forefront of every ministry of the Kingdom Church. The prophetic watchman and the prophetic intercessor is the same person interceding and co-laboring with the prayer warrior to fight for God's prophetic people and God's prophetic Church.

The Kingdom apostle fulfills the office of the Kingdom prophet and often enter into the apostolic prophetic inter-cession for God's heritage and God's work. The fullness of time has come for the 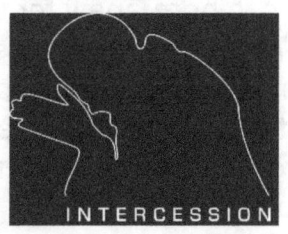 church to know that ministries and ministers are called to be Kingdom prophets to fulfill God's purpose for this Kingdom Age.

The prophetic intercessor's ministry is the prophetic ministry of the Kingdom, because the Kingdom prophet intercessor knows the seasons and time, and is now released in the church through intercession to birth the Church into it present-day season. Three requirements for anyone called to this awakening Church must be met--especially to the prophet and the intercessor. The three requirements for one prepared to walk in a Kingdom Office--especially the office of Kingdom prophet intercessor:

1. *Answer the call to Intercession to enter into one's ministry.*

2. *Allow the Lord to heal, deliver, and cleanse the corrupt nature.*

3. *Birth in one's Ministry.*

A cursory look at the three-fold preparation one called to walk in the Office of the *Kingdom prophet who is the intercessor:*

⟵→ Answer the call to Intercession. When one is called by God to fulfill an assignment for the Kingdom, one is born anew for that call, and one grows and lives by and through **Intercession** to enter in and understand the call. Ministers are birthed into their ministry through **Intercession**. Ministers, especially prophets, live and grow through **Intercession**. Paul admonished the Ephesians to be ...

> *"Praying always with all prayer and supplication in the Spirit, and watching thereunto with all perseverance and supplication for all saints;"* Ephesians 6:18

↪ **Allow the Lord to heal, and deliver, and cleanse the corrupt nature.** The Church is populated with crippled and wounded saints. They need healing. Many try to fulfill an assignment for heaven, but often are defeated because they are bruised and battered by the world and have not been healed. It is written...

> *"...he hath anointed me to preach the gospel to the poor; he hath sent me to heal the brokenhearted, to preach deliverance to the captives, and recovering of sight to the blind, to set at liberty them that are bruised,"* Luke 4:18

↪ **Birth in one's Ministry.** One must learn to travail as a woman in birth to learn the heart and mind of God. One must then travail as a woman in birth to bring forth what God ordains for this earth. It is written ...

> *"And I gave my heart to seek and search out by wisdom concerning all things that are done under heaven: this sore travail hath God given to the sons of man to be exercised therewith."* Ecclesiastes 1:13

BELIEVERS/SAINTS CANNOT AFFORD TO IGNORE THE THREE-FOLD KINGDOM CALL

One may fail any one of the three-fold steps for preparation for a Kingdom call; therefore, that one will not be ready for this **End-Time Battle**. As one answers the call to **Intercession**, that one may be catapulted by God into any one of Kingdom **Offices**--The office of the prophet is one of the important Kingdom Office Ministries. However, God will not choose one who has not been healed of all hurts from the past and cleansed of the corrupt nature.

It is only when one is healed and cleansed that one can birth in his/her Kingdom ministry. Although the **prophet intercessor** is trained to hear the voice of God, that one is also positioned for battle. One may be called to the Kingdom office of the apostle, prophet, evangelist, pastor or teacher, but intercession is at the forefront of every call because of the purpose of the call. It is written...

> *"For the perfecting of the saints, for the work of the ministry, for the edifying of the body of Christ:*
>
> *"Till we all come in the unity of the faith, and of the knowledge of the Son of God, unto a perfect man, unto the measure of the stature of the fullness of Christ:* Ephesians 4:12-13

The one who walks in the office of the prophet who is the intercessor must have the veil of darkness lifted between him/her and God. God does not want to be a mystery to the one who walks in this all-important Kingdom prophet Intercessor's office; therefore, intercession is the way to

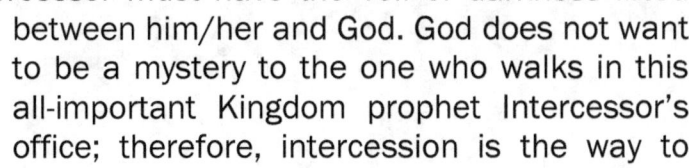

open communication between God and His called Kingdom prophet.

The prophets called to the office of the *Kingdom prophet who is the intercessor* must know God and acknowledge that which can only be obtained through personal, daily attendance upon God through a life of intercession. **The call to be the *Kingdom prophet who is the intercessor*** precedes the call to the office of Kingdom prophet, because the Kingdom intercessor is to be birthed into a spiritual place of battle as that one is birthed into his/her ministry.

The Kingdom prophet who is the intercessor called to the office of Kingdom prophet intercessor may or may not have an ecclesiastical collar at the onset of the call, or have been pointed to a ministerial office such as an **apostle** or **prophet**, etc. The *Kingdom prophet who is the intercessor* will be strategic in the battle to come, and, therefore, must be well prepared for the battle ahead.

The *Kingdom prophet who is the intercessor* comes to the doorway of the Kingdom age carrying two burdens— a burden for the end of the season and the burden for that which is to come. The *Kingdom prophet who is the intercessor*, therefore, will need to be prepared to manifest all the supernatural power needed for the harvest of souls that will be birthed into the Kingdom of God.

Chapter 2

THE KINGDOM PROPHET INTERCESSOR CARRIES TWO BURDENS FOR THE CHURCH

Because the *Kingdom prophet who is the intercessor* can see and know the seasons and times, that one sees the present day church and where it is. His/her intercessory prayer burden is for the church which is ill-prepared to arise into its Kingdom position. The other prayer burden the Kingdom prophet who is the intercessor carries is knowing, interceding, and trying to prepare the Church for that which is to come. Through the intercession of the prophet who is the intercessor, God is revealing those deep things which no man knows but God and those to whom He reveals them.

It is the prophet intercessor who will unfurl the glorious vision of the appearance of the Lord Jesus Christ as King and open the way for His entrance into the Church. The intercession of the *Kingdom prophet who is the intercessor* will uncover things which must shortly come to pass.

The Kingdom Prophet who is the intercessor has been hidden somewhat because his/her identity was cloaked in his/her role as pastor, as shepherd, as prophet, as apostle, as intercessor, or as prayer warrior. He is coming on the scene now to bear record of the Word of God and of the testimony of Jesus Christ as written in Revelation. It is written...

"The Revelation of Jesus Christ, which God gave unto him, to shew unto his servants things which

must shortly come to pass; and he sent and signified it by his angel unto his servant John:

"Who bare record of the word of God, and of the testimony of Jesus Christ, and of all things he saw." Revelation 1:1-2

In these last days, the prophet who stands in the forefront of the Kingdom age in his/her prophetic intercession, prophetic preaching and teaching speaks clearly of Christ the King, who He is and what He requires for entrance into the Kingdom. Some may venture to say that the Church has been doing what God required. The answer is yes, but much is still in the heart of God as to what is required for entrance into the Kingdom, and God is now ready to release these truths to the **Kingdom prophet who is the intercessor.**

It is at this juncture of the Church age that God sends the end-time Kingdom prophet to make known the things that shall be here after. That is why prophets are called to be prophet intercessors just as the end-time Kingdom apostle is more than an Apostle.

The prophets of old, Ezekiel, Isaiah, Malachi, Jeremiah, etc. were prophets. The apostle is also an intercessor chosen to establish through Kingdom apostolic intercession what the King is speaking through divine revelation of the Kingdom. The Apostle Paul was an intercessor. It is written...

"For this cause I bow my knees unto the Father of our Lord Jesus Christ,

> *"Of whom the whole family in heaven and earth is named,"* Ephesians 3:14-15

The Apostle Paul also taught and called all of his subjects to intercession. It is written...

> *"And take the helmet of salvation, and the sword of the Spirit, which is the word of God:*
>
> *"Praying always with all prayer and supplication in the Spirit, and watching thereunto with all perseverance and supplication for all saints."* Ephesians 6:17-18

The fullness of time has come for intercessors to come forth and know that they are prepared for this Kingdom age. Even the evangelist is called to the office of **Kingdom prophet who is the intercessor.** The ones walking in a Five-fold office have carved a space in the spiritual realm to stand in intercession during the years of their fulfilling the call of their office. They are positioned to stand before the King because they are sanctified to serve the King and bring the message to the Church.

As prophecy gives an account of things to come, the one called to the office of the **Kingdom prophet who is the intercessor** will reveal future events in a way that will reveal that which is God's wisdom and God's holy purposes. The preparation of the Kingdom prophet intercessor has been ongoing for some time, but many are called but few are chosen. The call has always been there for the prophets to be the intercessor of the day, but now the call is loud and clear—come forth as the catalyst for church to arise.

Why is the call so loud and clear today for the ones called to the office of *Kingdom prophet who is the intercessor?* Perhaps it is because it is a call to release revelation of things of what is to come to pass very soon. As the prophet intercessor and the apostolic intercessor work together, the church will be awakened to the fact that God is ready to establish His purposes for the Kingdom church.

Be it known that the one called to the office of Kingdom intercessor will bear record of the word of God and of the testimony of Jesus. The Lord needs not only the prophet to hear what is in the heart of God and bring it to the church, but the apostolic intercessor needs to touch the Heart of God in intercession in order to be quick to establish on earth what He/she receives in intercession. All or much of what will be done to establish the Kingdom Church is in the heart of God.

The one walking in the office of Kingdom prophet intercessor will not and cannot bear record of his/her invention or imagination. All must be and will be the record of God and the testimony of Jesus Christ. The training and preparation of a *Kingdom prophet who is the intercessor* has been intense and sure. The training had a strategic purpose. It was to cause the church to arise to its Kingdom position.

The called *Kingdom prophet who is the intercessor* was prepared well in the furnace of fire of the Lord as they were trained in the prophetic and in intercession. They are prepared so well in the furnace of fire that they know that every word they receive from the King is sacred, and that nothing should be added or nothing changed.

Seared in the heart of the **Kingdom prophet who is the intercessor** is the truth that the time is at hand, and the church should be so much the more attentive to see the day approaching for the Kingdom to come on earth as it is in heaven. The prepared **Kingdom prophet who is the intercessor** knows that the Lord has released unto that one the awesome task of changing the face of the Church so that the King can come in and do exploits; that is, to fulfill His purpose for dying on the cross.

A clarion call is being issued from the throne of God for the Kingdom Prophet who is the Kingdom intercessor to come forth and stand in the gap for theEnd-Time Kingdom church to arise. The strategic training and preparation for the office of the prophet is in intercession. Many who are called to the office of the prophet are not chosen because they bypassed the rudimentary training of intercession.

The steps to preparation for the prophetic ministry are:

1. Answer the call to the ministry of intercession for the prophetic ministry. That means that one puts the call to the prophet on the altar and answers the call to intercession.
2. If one answers the call to a Kingdom office and does not allow the Lord to heal and deliver from the corrupt nature, that one fails at that point. As that one sinks deeper into intercession, forgetting all else, that one will be healed, and self and the corrupt nature will ebb away.

3. Birth in one's true ministry. Prayer, intercession and travail, which one has been sanctified in by entering fully into Step 1 and Step 2 above, will birth in one's Kingdom ministry.

Why the intense preparation for the ministry office of the *Kingdom prophet who is the intercessor?* Special preparation is needed because it is a special office for special people who are brought forth for a special purpose. This is a ministry for people who are being made according to God's pattern for God's glory. This ministry to the office of the prophet is as the landing strip is to an airplane. A plane that has been flying and flying needs a landing strip and welcomes that landing strip when flying time is ever. Intercession is the landing strip for *Kingdom prophet who is the intercessor.*

The call to the office of *Kingdom prophet who is the intercessor* is not a call to beginners to go out and begin tomorrow. It is not a popular call. It is a call to a special office for those specially called by God, separated unto God, brought forth by God, appointed and anointed by God Himself for a time like this. It is the call of and the call to the office of the Kingdom prophet.

The call to the *Kingdom prophet who is the intercessor* is a call to the office of a *Kingdom prophet who is the intercessor* in the Church, the Body of Christ for the Church, and in the world today. It is a call to enter into the ministry of intercession which leads to prophetic ministry which requires consecrated listening to God and dedicated prophetic work for God. The prophets of the Old Testament were intercessors. How else could they speak God's Word?

The prophetic call on today's prophets is the call of the office *Kingdom prophet who is the intercessor* and is a call like no other call. The *Kingdom prophet who is the intercessor* is one whose mouth has been touched and prepared to speak for God as Isaiah, the embodiment of a prophet intercessor. It is written ...

> *"Then said I, Woe is me! for I am undone; because I am a man of unclean lips, and I dwell in the midst of a people of unclean lips: for mine eyes have seen the King, the LORD of hosts.*
>
> *"Then flew one of the seraphims unto me, having a live coal in his hand, which he had taken with the tongs from off the altar:*
>
> *"And he laid it upon my mouth, and said, Lo, this hath touch thy lips; and thine iniquity is taken away, and thy sin purged."* Isaiah 6:5-7

A study of Isaiah and the other prophets of the Old Testament reveal them to be Kingdom prophets who were intercessors made according to God's pattern. It also reveals the heavy price the ones paid whose mouth had been touched by God to speak for Him. Their lives and works reveal the heavy price one must pay today for the power of that touch. Much of, or maybe all, that work is the work of intercession.

The call to the office of the *Kingdom prophet who is the intercessor* is the call to be a watchman upon the wall for God Almighty. The tasks of watchman upon the walls of the city, the city of God's people, God's church—the Body of Christ--is a task which claims the Kingdom prophet intercessor's life completely. That is why the death blow must kill all of the self-life before one passes through the door of the prophet who is the intercessor.

The very life of the called and established *Kingdom prophet who is the intercessor* belongs to God for God moves and acts through the "called out" prophet intercessor; therefore, that one's very life and breath is intercession within the church, for the Church. At this critical time in Church history, the office of the prophet who is the intercessor is needed to open the way for the Kingdom to come into the Church. This will cause the Church to awaken and arise to its Kingdom position.

The Body of Christ is hurting for the true prophet who is the intercessor. The Lord is now making a clarion call for the true prophet who is the intercessor. The Spirit is **saying "...in with the true prophet who is the intercessor, out with the pseudo prophet."** The plague of the Body of Christ today is the pseudo prophets who are seeking out Holy Ghost servants of God and Holy Ghost Churches believing they have a word from the Lord. God does, however, want to give them His word, but they must allow the Lord to bring them to the end of themselves.

The true *Kingdom prophet who is the intercessor* is brought forth by God in the Church, the Body of Christ and for the Church, the Body of Christ. Many of the pseudo prophets stand on their own platform speaking forth their own word instead of God's. They have not been trained in the furnace of God's fire and are, therefore, giving out "strange fire." These beloved ones love the office of the prophet, but have not found their way through the door of preparation for the office.

Some of the pseudo prophets may have been called to be prophets, but have not spent the necessary time before God in powerful personal intercession and quiet waiting before the Lord which leads to cleansing and healing and deliverance to hear a clear call from God. They have not been made according to His pattern.

Often, the pseudo prophets have not surrendered their lives to the Lord. Often, they do not know the meaning of total unconditional surrender to the Lord — If this fundamental condition has not been met, how then can they be true *Kingdom prophets who are the intercessors?* These dear ones then become a menace to the body of Christ because they are like loose cannons ready to explode wherever the devil sees fit. May they allow the Lord to apprehend them and carry them through the furnace of fire.

Pause Here and Read This Special Note

If you are reading this book, the call to be the Kingdom prophet who is the intercessor is for you, not someone else. It is a call that will bring one to the sum total of all that one has learned in his/her Christian experience. One may continue reading to the end of the book. However, after the first reading one should reread each chapter as suggested below for the King to open the way for one to be brought into the Office.

Take as much time as necessary to prepare to accept the Kingdom call to the Ministry of the Kingdom prophet who is the intercessor.

> This Call to the *Kingdom prophet who is the intercessor* is for anyone who will say "yes" to the call.

Spend one week or more with each chapter of this book as follows:

1. Spend one week or more reading, praying, each chapter. Read a paragraph, then think on the fact of that chapter, then pray the paragraph asking the Lord about the contents of the paragraph or to give His mind on the paragraph or to make what is written in the paragraph available to you.

2. Obtain a special journal or notebook and make notes of what the Lord reveals. Whatever He says to do, just do it before going on to the next chapter.

Chapter 3

> **THE MAKING OF A *KINGDOM PROPHET***
> **WHO IS THE *INTERCESSOR***

The office of the **Kingdom prophet who is the *intercessor*** is set forth in the Old Testament because the prophets of the Old Testament were prophets who were the intercessors. This Kingdom office finds its fulfillment in the New Testament. One sees the call and making of the prophet who is the intercessor in the Old Testament for Major Prophets. One can then understand better the call now to the office of Kingdom prophet for the present New Testament Church. Notice Isaiah's call:

> *"And he said, Go, and tell this people, Hear ye indeed, but understand not; and see ye indeed, but perceive not.*
>
> *"Make the heart of this people fat, and make their ears heavy, and shut their eyes; lest they see with their eyes, and hear with their ears, and understand with their heart, and convert, and be healed."*
> Isaiah 6:9-10

As one reads the book of Isaiah, one sees the making of a Kingdom prophet who is a special "called out" prophet who is the intercessor operating in a special office. One sees Isaiah enduring suffering for the Lord and hardships which befall one who is called to this office. One sees these special "called out" ones obeying and overcoming, but experiencing that intimate walk with God Himself as only a ***prophet who is the intercessor experiences.***

Note the call of Jeremiah . . .

> "Then the word of the LORD came unto me, saying,
>
> "Before I formed thee in the belly I knew thee; and before thou camest forth out of the womb I sanctified thee, and I ordained thee a prophet unto the nations." Jeremiah 1:4-5

Note the call of Ezekiel . . .

> "And he said unto me, Son of man, stand upon thy feet, and I will speak unto thee.
>
> "And the spirit entered into me when he spake unto me, and set me upon my feet, that I heard him that spake onto me.
>
> "And he said unto me, Son of man, I send thee to the children of Israel, to a rebellious nation that hath rebelled against me: they and their fathers have transgressed against me, even unto this very day." Ezekiel 2:1-3

One can see clearly that the call to the office of **Kingdom prophet who is the intercessor** is clearly illustrated in the life and work of Ezekiel. The book of Ezekiel presents a clear picture of the training preparation and the making of a prophet. It is in the book of Ezekiel that God reveals himself as Jehovah Shammah—God is there. In the last chapter of the book of Ezekiel where it is used in reference to the earthly Jerusalem, the city which the Lord Jesus will inhabit when he returns to the earth to reign as King of Kings, and Lord of Lord. This was the ministry of a Kingdom prophet who was the intercessor.

It is written...

"...and the name of the City from that day shall be, the LORD is there." Ezekiel 48:35

The word is simply the word for "there," and the name Jehovah Shammah describes the character of God as "there," meaning that He is there. The prophet who walks in the office of a *Kingdom prophet who is the intercessor* will know Him as Jehovah Shammah because He will be there. When God revealed himself as Jehovah Shammah in Ezekiel 48:35, He named the city of Jerusalem Shammah, thereby, assuring His people that He, Jehovah, would be there.

As one moves into the office of the *Kingdom prophet who is the intercessor,* the Lord is and will be there always. When one refers to God as Jehovah Shammah, one is simply saying "God is there." The one reading this needs to know and believe that God is there/here and that He is issuing this call to anyone who is willing to become His prophet who is the intercessor.

The Higher Call of the Kingdom Prophet
Why the call for the restoration of the prophet?

Prophets and prophecy were the guiding force before the coming of Christ. God did not do away with prophets, and prophecy did not cease with the coming of Jesus when the church was born. Instead the office took on new meaning and became more multifaceted. God expanded the office, and the function and power of the prophetic calling, when Jesus died and rose again.

One sees Jesus Christ in the office of a true Prophet and Intercessor as He brings forth the Prophetic Word. When Jesus was on earth, His entire life was spent leading, guiding, teaching, and preparing a prophetic people. One sees Him as intercessor, especially in John 17—interceding for the ones given to Him as a prophetic people. Because of Jesus Christ and  what He did, the prophet who is the Intercessor today is not a lonely watchman as in the Old Testament prophet often put to death because of the prophetic Word.

Today the **Kingdom prophet who is the intercessor** may not be put to death but may endure the suffering of being misunderstood, and persecuted by the Church, and the Body of Christ. The suffering may occur because the Church, the Body of Christ may not understand nor recognize the role of the prophet intercessor, nor recognize that the prophet who is the intercessor today is to be an integral part of the Church.

The **Kingdom prophet who is the intercessor** must know that he/she is not a lone ranger going in to give a word from God, but not connected to the church and to others flowing in the Kingdom ministries of the Church. Both the Church and the called *Kingdom prophet who is the intercessor* must acknowledge their marriage to one another.

The Church often may not understand the integral role of the prophet who is the intercessor in the church; therefore, the prophet who is the intercessor may endure much suffering at the hand of those for whom he/she is called to stand as a watchman. Nevertheless, the prophet who is the intercessor is to stand as that watchman and as that intercessor, and as that guide to prepare God's Church, the Body of Christ for Christ. It is written...

> *"That he might sanctify and cleanse it with the washing of water by the word,*
>
> *"That he might present it to himself a glorious church, not having spot or wrinkle, or any such thing; but that it should be holy and without blemish."* Ephesians 5:26-27

THE COST OF ANSWERING THE CALL OF THE *KINGDOM PROPHET WHO IS THE INTERCESSOR*

The Prophet call to the ministry of the *Kingdom prophet who is the intercessor* is a costly call, and one needs to count the cost. As in no other call, the Lord calls but will not bring one into this office until one says "yes." This is not an office where one is deposited as a result of salvation. This is a call issued by God Himself to one brought forth and made according to God's pattern. God calls, however, but awaits the one called to say "yes" to the call. God said in making the call known to Isaiah...

> "Also, I heard the voice of the Lord saying, whom shall I send, and who shall go for us?..." Isaiah 6:8

Isaiah had to choose to answer that call. God could have constrained him to go, but he waited for Isaiah to say 'yes'. *"...Then said I, here am I; send me."* Isaiah 6:8

It was then that God accepted Isaiah as a *Prophet who was an intercessor* and told him what to do. His lips had been touched by God just before God said **"whom shall we send ..."** Then he could be sent to speak for God....

> "And he said, Go, and tell this people, Hear ye indeed, but understand not; and see ye indeed, but perceive not.
>
> "Make the heart of this people fat, and make their ears heavy, and shut their eyes; lest they see with their eyes, and hear with their ears, and understand with their heart, and convert, and be healed."
> Isaiah 6:9-10

Spend one week or more reading and praying the preceding chapter as follows in order to become the Kingdom prophet who is the intercessor.

Read a paragraph, then think on the fact of the paragraph, then pray the paragraph asking the Lord about the contents of the paragraph.

Make what is written in the paragraph yours.
Write what He says to do, and just do it.

Chapter 4

THE OFFICE OF THE KINGDOM PROPHET INTERCESSOR REQUIRES A SPECIAL DEATH TO SELF

The preparation for the *Kingdom prophet who is the intercessor* must include death to self in the fullest sense of the word. The end-time *Kingdom prophet who is the intercessor* just as the *Kingdom prophet who is the intercessor* of the Old Testament cannot speak on his own and has absolutely no power in self. For that reason, the *Kingdom prophet who is the intercessor* must be cleansed thoroughly, healed, delivered, and completely dead to self. This includes everything good, noble and right in his/her sight, and everything God puts His finger on before entering into this office.

All that the *Kingdom prophet who is the intercessor* does is done by the Holy Spirit power. The Kingdom prophet who is the intercessor is the prophet of today who is called to prepare God's prophetic people through the mighty power of the Holy Spirit for that great  day they are to enter in that new city of Jerusalem. The body of Christ needs the *Kingdom prophet who is the intercessor* more than ever today because much preparation is needed for God's people to be ready for the coming of the King.

Just as God in the Old Testament time called forth prophets as watchmen upon the wall to warn the people before He acted, the Lord is calling forth Kingdom watchmen to warn His Prophetic People before what needs to be set in order for the coming of the King. Today more than ever God's Prophetic People needs the watchman upon the walls. It is written

> "...watchman upon thy walls...which shall never hold their peace day nor night...
>
> "And give him no rest, till he establish, and till he make Jerusalem a praise in the earth."
> Isaiah 62:6-7

The Body of Christ—God's People—the Church now needs the *Kingdom prophet who is the intercessor* to prepare them and to get them ready for the close of the age. The *Kingdom prophet who is the intercessor* is needed to interpret the Bible and give fresh revelation with new life from a living God and intercede for the people as they often choke on the revelation. That is the job of the *Kingdom prophet who is the intercessor*.

The mouth of the *Kingdom prophet who is the intercessor* must be touched by God to speak for God; therefore, the *Kingdom prophet who is the intercessor* is to know that the word of God is utterly true and cannot be broken. Therefore, the *Kingdom prophet who is the intercessor* maintains his/her position of power through a deep, intimate walk with God in Prayer and the Word of God for God's Prophetic People. He/she can have no doubt regarding God and His word because the Kingdom prophet who is the intercessor lives for God and by God and will die for God and God's Word.

The word of the *Kingdom prophet who is the intercessor* is God's word of opening the way of the Lord for the Prophetic People of God--The Lord commands and the *Kingdom prophet who is the intercessor* opens the way of the Lord. Because of the death to self of the *Kingdom prophet who is the intercessor*'s self, he/she can open the waters of life to the church, for the church, and to individuals. Out of that one's death to self, God's plan and purpose for His Prophetic People can come forth.

The great power God must give to the *Kingdom prophet who is the intercessor* to do the great work of preparing and guiding God's Prophetic People is not given lightly or without the price of dying that one's death to self. The cost to the *Kingdom prophet who is the intercessor* is that one exchanges his/her life for the life of the King. Only through complete death to self can the *Kingdom prophet who is the intercessor* listen and obey God, and if one fails, God will raise up another.

The *Kingdom prophet who is the intercessor* has much putting off and putting on to do--Much cleansing and healing must take place in that one's life. One's innermost being is the reservoir of the power of the Holy Spirit, but much debris may have hindered the work of the Holy Spirit in and through the one called.

The Heart may have been a cesspool for many years for satan's debris. However, a powerful waterfall is waiting to burst forth from within when all is set right inside. Yes, out of one's belly will flow living waters when all the work on the inside is done that needs to be done, and the 'greening of the gorge' begins.

Some Work to be done on the inside so that the 'Greening of the Gorge' can begin

Finally, the Lord God Almighty is within every saint/believer a waiting that one's **'yes'** answer so that he can cleanse that one so that His dammed up power will have free course to burst forth, move and operate through him/her. The call is to begin today. Note the following illustration.

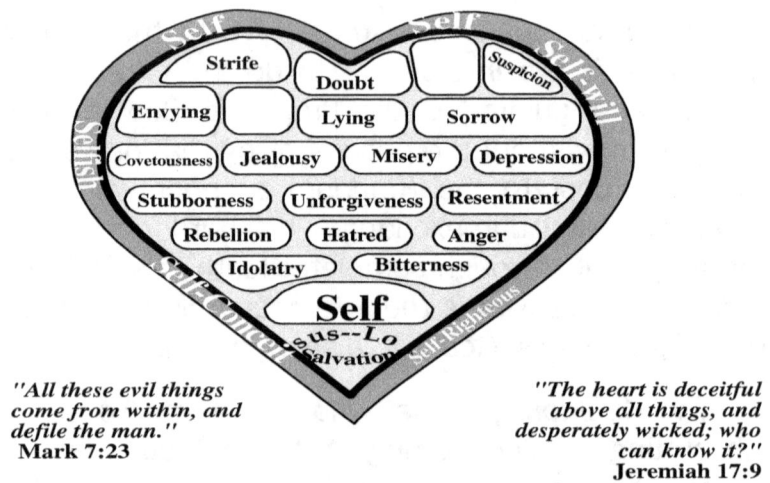

"All these evil things come from within, and defile the man."
Mark 7:23

"The heart is deceitful above all things, and desperately wicked; who can know it?"
Jeremiah 17:9

This Heart needs the 'greening of the gorge.'

NOW THE CALL GOES OUT TO THE PROPHETIC CHURCH

When one says 'yes' to the call to be the *Kingdom prophet who is the intercessor*, training begins. Discipline, training, and chastisement are required for the *Kingdom prophet who is the intercessor*. The *Kingdom prophet who is the intercessor*, more than all others, must die to self every day. If one says 'yes' to this great call, that one's work is not his/her own. The Lord decides and teaches as that one experiences trial and error. As one says 'yes' to the call and enter into the call, he/she may be persecuted, laughed at and rejected. However, he/she will arise, maybe to fail again and again, until that one cries out like Nebuchadnezzar. It is written...

> *"...Most High ruleth in the kingdom of men and giveth it to whomsoever he will."* Daniel 4:32

The call is clear now to anyone willing to take this death walk into God, to one willing to give up all claim to life and allow the Lord to bring him/her into death and resurrection of self to arise to walk with him in newness of life. Many who believe that they are called to be a prophet have perhaps been a distant follower of Jesus the multitude Jesus as inspoke to in Luke 14.

The multitudes followed Jesus, and He turned to them and told them the requirements for being a true follower. It is written...

> *"And there went great multitudes with him: and he turned, and said...*
>
> *"If any man come to me, and hate not his father, and mother, and wife, and children, and brethren, and sisters, yea, and his own life also, he cannot be my disciple.*
>
> *"And whosoever doth not bear his cross, and come after me, cannot be my disciple.*
>
> *"For which of you, intending to build a tower, sitteth not down first, and counteth the cost, whether he have sufficient to finish it?*

"Lest haply, after he hath laid the foundation, and is not able to finish it, all that behold it begin to mock him,

"Saying, This man began to build, and was not able to finish.

"Or what king, going to make war against another king, sitteth not down first, and consulteth whether he be able with ten thousand to meet him that cometh against him with twenty thousand?

"Or else, while the other is yet a great way off, he sendeth an ambassage, and desireth conditions of peace.

"so likewise, whosoever he be of you that forsaketh not all that he hath, he cannot be my disciple."
Luke 14:25-33

Do you believe that you have been called to be a prophet? Have you been giving a word of prophesy here and there in the Church? Know that does not make one a **Kingdom prophet who is the intercessor.** Perhaps one has been walking with the Lord for a long time and maybe working in the ministry, but that does not make one the **Kingdom prophet who is the intercessor.** Many of these are as the multitudes as in Luke 14.

What he said to the multitude (remember the multitudes were with Him) he says to the called one today. In his saying he lays the foundation for the fundamental calling of the **Kingdom prophet who is the intercessor.** This scripture outlines the price of this calling. One must forsake all to become the *Kingdom prophet who is the intercessor.*

ACCEPTANCE TO THE CALL TO BE THE *KINGDOM* PROPHET WHO IS THE INTERCESSOR

The *Kingdom prophet who is the intercessor* has much studying to do and much praying to do. The Lord calls you to do as Ezekiel.

> *"...Son of man, eat that thou findest; eat this roll, and go speak unto the house of Israel.*
>
> *"So I opened my mouth and he caused me to eat that roll.*
>
> *"And he said unto me, Son of man, cause thy belly to eat and fill thy bowels with this roll that I give thee. Then did I eat it; and it was in my mouth as honey for sweetness."* Ezekiel 3:1-3

Unless one is willing to give yourself to consistent prayer and consistent and structured study of God's word, that one cannot and will not be used effectively by God in any office, and definitely will not be called by God to serve in the office of the *Kingdom prophet who is the intercessor.* Know that much prayer, travailing prayer, leads to the prophetic work.

If one believes God has called him/her to this special office, that one must choose to commit self to a special time daily — at least one hour of prayer three times a week and Bible study. One can do it, something may have to be sacrificed — maybe sleep, maybe TV, maybe friends, maybe church work—that is outside one's calling. Just know that when one says 'yes', God will show that one what must be done and He will do it.

The **Kingdom prophet who is the intercessor** has much putting off and putting on to do. Much cleansing and healing must take place because that one's innermost being is to be prepared to be a place of abode of the power of the Holy Ghost. A great power is waiting to burst forth from within when all is prepared inside.

The one who believes that he/she has been called for the ministry of the **Kingdom prophet who is the intercessor** should seek the Lord for the preparation for this great calling. If the call is sure and one's answer is 'yes,' that one must then allow God to make him/her according to His pattern to be the **Kingdom prophet who is the intercessor.**

When the work that needs to be worked on the inside of the **Kingdom prophet who is the intercessor** is completed, the "greening of the gorge" begins. The Lord God Almighty is within that one awaiting the 'yes' answer so that the Lord can begin the cleansing will begin the work inside the called Kingdom prophet.

When the cleansing is complete, The Lord's dammed-up power will have free course to burst forth, move and operate through the **Kingdom prophet who is the intercessor.** The first call is for the one called is to....

> *"...put off concerning the former conversation the old man, which is corrupt according to the deceitful lusts;*
>
> *"And be renewed in the spirit of your mind;*

"And that ye put on the new man, which after God is created in righteousness and true holiness."
Ephesians 4:22-24

Some Kingdom prophets may have been a while in the making, but that one will enter into some more making in order to be made according to God's pattern. That one truly will be made according to God's pattern if he/she is to be a *Kingdom prophet who is the intercessor.* If one is willing to say 'yes' to the great calling of the Lord, he/she must enter into covenant for this great calling. It is written...

"Now unto him that is able to do exceeding abundantly above all that we ask or think, according to the power that worketh in us.

"Unto him be glory in the church by Christ Jesus throughout all ages, world without end. Amen."
Ephesians 3:20-21

Pause Here and pray for entrance into the Office of the Kingdom prophet Intercessor

Spend one week or more reading and praying the preceding chapter as follows in order to become the *Kingdom prophet who is the intercessor.*

Read a paragraph, then think on the fact of the paragraph, then pray the paragraph asking the Lord about the contents of the paragraph or to make what is written in the paragraph yours. Write what He says to do, and just do it.

OFTENTIMES ONE MAY NEED HEALING OF HURTS FROM THE PAST. THE FOLLOWING IS A PRAYER FOR HEALING OF THE MIND AND HEART.

PRACTICAL EXERCISE FOR HEALING OF THE MIND AND HEART

When one considers the many ways Satan has set to block the believer, it becomes apparent that one must be very serious about his/her own healing and deliverance from bondage, because Satan is still at work to keep the believer from dwelling in the presence of the Lord.

Jesus Christ is the healer, and the believer in Jesus Christ can know that *"...greater is he that is in you, than he that is in the world."* (I John 4:4) Healing, therefore, is for the believer in Jesus Christ.

To complete the following exercise, meet with the Lord at least three times a week, or every day. You will need your Bible and a prayer notebook.

This is a three-week exercise, but it may take longer. Meet with the Lord three times a week for about 30 minutes for the three weeks to complete this exercise, but if you don't think that your mind has been healed, continue as long as necessary. It is very important that you follow directions as given and that the exercise is completed in the Spirit.

*** **PSALM 51** will be used to heal your mind. The word of God is your medicine, but you must take it as directed.

***   Each time you meet with the Lord, read Psalm 51 out loud three times.

First Reading: Read slowly but read without stopping.

Second Reading: Read slowly again, but this time pause after each verse and think on the verse. If your mind is damaged in any way, you may have a difficult time focusing or understanding. Try anyway and keep trying.

Third Reading: Read slowly again. This time stop after each verse and pray the verse for yourself.

After the Third Reading, take a verse each time beginning with verse 1 and read it out loud three times, pausing after each reading to think on the verse. Pray that verse and try to memorize the verse.

Finally, write anything in your prayer notebook which God reveals to you about a verse or verses from Psalm 51.

Practical Exercise For Healing of The Heart

(Please don't begin this exercise until you have completed the previous exercise for healing of the mind.)

Please don't rush through this exercise. You are to meet with the Lord at least three times a week for another two weeks, and pray the following scriptural prayer out loud each time you meet with the Lord. Pray slowly and think on what you are praying.

The following scriptural prayer is taken from Psalm 25. You may want to pray it as written here or you may want to take your Bible and pray it your way — please use Psalm 25. If you pray this prayer, read Psalm 25 through from your Bible once a week.

Dear Father, I come in the Name of Jesus ...

Unto thee, O Lord, do I lift up my soul. My soul is corrupt, and my heart is broken. I have been bruised and battered inside, and my pain is deep — so deep that it is somewhat hidden from me, but I know it is not hidden from you.

O my God, I trust in thee ... let me not be ashamed, let not my enemies triumph over me. Satan has set up much against me, but I wait on you for my help.

Yea, let none that wait on thee be ashamed: let them be ashamed which transgress without cause.

Show me thy ways, O Lord; teach me thy paths. I lost my way as a child, and so many things have happened to me that I am locked up inside. Lead me in thy truth, and teach me: for thou art the God of my salvation; on thee do I wait all the day.

Remember, O Lord, thy tender mercies, and thy loving kindness; for they have been ever of old.

Remember not the sins of my youth, nor my transgressions: according to thy mercy remember thou me for thy goodness sake, O Lord. Remember not the bitterness, the anger, the unforgiveness, the resentment of my youth, nor any of the other sins of my youth.

Good and upright is the Lord; therefore, will he teach sinners in the way. I know that I have sinned in my heart, but you will teach me.

All the paths of the Lord are mercy and truth unto such as keep his covenant and his testimonies. Lord, I need your mercy and truth. I need truth in the inward parts, and I need wisdom in the hidden parts. I need to know the truth that the truth can make me free.

For thy name's sake, O Lord, pardon mine iniquity; for it is great. I have held unforgiveness against others. Please forgive me.

What man is he that feareth the Lord? Him shall He teach in the way that He shall choose. Lord, I fear thee, but I am not sure I fear thee right. Please instill in me a holy fear of you and teach me in the way that you choose.

It is written that "His soul shall dwell at ease; and his seed shall inherit the earth." Please let my soul dwell at ease and let my seed inherit the earth.

The secret of the Lord is with them that fear him; and he will show them his covenant. Lord, mine eyes are ever toward Thee for you shall pluck my feet out of the net.

Lord, the memories from the past, the pain, the hurt, all have ensnared me like a net. Turn Thee unto me, and have mercy upon me; for I am desolate and afflicted.

The troubles of my heart are enlarged: O, bring thou me out of my distresses.

Look upon mine affliction and my pain; and forgive all my sins. Consider mine enemies; for they are many; and they hate me with cruel hatred.

Let integrity and uprightness preserve me; for I wait on Thee. Redeem me, O God, out of all my troubles. AMEN

Each time you pray this prayer, stop after each paragraph and think on the words of the prayer. After you pray the prayer, quietly wait before the Lord to give Him time to speak to your heart, and in your prayer notebook, write what comes to your heart and mind.

PART II

The Doorway to...

...THE WORK OF THE KINGDOM PROPHET
...WHO IS THE INTERCESSION

Preparation for...

THE KINGDOM PROPHET WHO IS
THE INTERCESSOR

The call to become...

It is written...

"For ye are dead, and your life is hid with Christ in God."
Colossians 3:3

Chapter 5

INTERCESSION BRINGS UNDERSTANDING OF THE PROPHETIC ASSIGNMENT

The ministry of the *Kingdom prophet who is the intercessor* brings one into an intimate relationship with the King. In that intimate relationship, the *Kingdom prophet who is the intercessor* comes to understand the great power and the awesome privilege being given the assignment to tusher in the Kingdom through intercession.

In the work of Kingdom intercession the prophet learns from the *King* that God is his/her Father and the Father of the Lord Jesus Christ who is King of kings and Lord of lords. It is there that one receives not only the prophetic word from God, but also grace and peace to fulfill the assignment. It is written...

> *"Grace be to you, and peace, from God our Father, and from the Lord Jesus Christ.*
>
> *"Blessed be the God and Father of our Lord Jesus Christ, who hath blessed us with all spiritual blessings in heavenly places in Christ:"* Eph. 1:2-3

In the ministry of Kingdom intercession, the *Kingdom prophet who is the intercessor* can trust that God the Father will act on his/her behalf. The intercession brings the prophet to trust that God will answer prayers and that God will fulfill the work he/she brings to the Church. When the Kingdom prophet comes in close to the King in intercession, the prophetic word he/she gives passes from his/her mouth into the hands of the King for fulfillment. He then assumes the responsibility to fulfill that prophetic word.

In the Kingdom prophetic ministry of intercession as one waits on and abides in the Lord, that one enters into the ministry of prayer that leads to intercession for the King. The ministry of prayer that leads to intercession is the special ministry where the one praying is positioned by the King to carry out the will of God of the universe, and Jesus takes the prophet's prayers to the Father. It is written...

> *"...this man, (Jesus) because he continueth ever, hath an unchangeable priesthood.*
>
> *"Wherefore he is able also to save them to the uttermost that come unto God by Him, seeing he ever liveth to make intercession for them."* Heb. 7:24-25

THE KINGDOM PROPHET WHO IS THE INTERCESSOR HAS A DEEPER UNDERSTANDING OF THE KINGDOM

A closer view of the call to be a **Kingdom prophet who is the intercessor** brings one to see and understand the call and purpose of the prophetic. The **Kingdom prophet who is the intercessor** has been given a special assignment in God's Prophetic Movement; therefore, this prophet needs to know the meaning of the Word...

> *"... ye are a chosen generation, a royal priesthood, an holy nation, a peculiar people; that ye should show forth the praises of him who hath called you out of darkness into his marvelous light."* I Peter 2:9

In this world of burgeoning prophets, many of whom feel and know the call to intercession is issued to them, too many will give no credence to having to stop by way of spending time with Christ in His school for preparation for this awesome call. Too many are ready to plunge headlong into the call without this much-needed time in preparation. They need to understand the time of preparation is to bring them into the hidden place with the King that gives them the Kingdom word for the Kingdom Church.

The Kingdom word for the Kingdom Church is a word beyond the prophetic word of comfort, promise, and love and care. Those much needed words will be given, but will be inextricably interwoven in words to bring a prophetic people into the prophetic move of God.

What one who avoids the preparation time required for preparing to becoming hidden with Christ in God does not realize is that this preparation determines whether he/she will enter in and remain God's **Kingdom prophet who is the intercessor**. The call to be a **Kingdom prophet who is the intercessor** prepares the prophet for a hidden life; that is, a life to be the *Hidden One* for the King, who is called to...

> *"...seek those things which are above, where Christ sitteth on the right hand of God.*
>
> *"Set your affection on things above, not on things on the earth.*
>
> *"For ye are dead, and your life is hid with Christ in God."* Colossians 3:1-3

The King is about the business of preparing the *Kingdom prophet who is the intercessor* for his/her role as Kingdom Prophet. The *Kingdom prophet who is the intercessor,* therefore, must be truly a *Hidden One* serving around the Throne of God constantly in the ministry of intercession.

The *Kingdom prophet who is the intercessor* must know the power in the Name of Jesus because this service is carried out all in the name of the Lord Jesus, the King. The prepared *Kingdom prophet who is the intercessor* has that power in his/her being and can release when and as the King directs.

Special Note

> This Call to the *Kingdom prophet who is the intercessor* is for anyone who will say "yes" to the call.

Spend one week or more with each chapter of this book as follows:

1. *Spend one week or more reading, praying, each chapter. Read a paragraph, then think on the fact of that chapter, then pray the paragraph asking the Lord about the contents of the paragraph or to give His mind on the paragraph or to make what is written in the paragraph available to you.*

2. *Obtain a special journal or notebook and make notes of what the Lord reveals. Whatever He says do, just do it before going on to the next chapter.*

CHAPTER 6

THE ROLE OF THE "HIDDEN ONES"

The *Kingdom prophet who is the intercessor* will receive from the King hidden truth to release to the church that has not been hidden from the church but truth hidden for the church. This is truth that has been hidden in the heart of God that God will give to the *Kingdom prophet who is the intercessor* to release to the church. This truth has been hidden for Kingdom purposes and needed a prepared *Kingdom prophet who is the intercessor* to release it to the church.

The *Kingdom prophet who is the intercessor* is called to the *"Inner Life"* to learn the deeper secrets of the Kingdom—The secrets hidden in the heart of God. This is *the why* of the call to the prophet to be a Hidden One with God. It is where Christ will bring one into the calling of the *Kingdom prophet who is the intercessor*—A call for which every prophet has been set apart.

To become a *"Hidden One for the Lord"* is the call for every Kingdom prophet and every believer. It is the call to intercession that prepares one to be the *Kingdom prophet who is the intercessor*. This is the call issued to the present-day prophet. If the prophet does not answer that call to intercession, the Lord reaches down and touches the heart of the one who is willing to make intercession his/her ministry because out of the school of intercession comes the *Kingdom prophet who is the intercessor.*

The *Hidden One* is the one who has said "yes" to the call to be the *Kingdom prophet who is the intercessor* and 'yes' to this hidden life with the Lord. That one can then be delivered out of the hand of the enemy on every front. It is written...

> *"...that we being delivered out of the hand of our enemies might serve him without fear,*
>
> *"In holiness and righteousness before him, all the days of our life."* Luke 1:74-75

The Hidden One, who says 'yes' to the call to be the *Kingdom prophet who is the intercessor* is saying 'yes' to a life where he/she will sit with Christ in heavenly places. It is a life where that one will remain forever hid with Christ in God. In that position, there can be no mixture; that is no flesh and no human work, because human effort is not permitted.

In the hidden place with God where the *Kingdom prophet who is the intercessor* lives and moves, God is all in all. There God alone is pre-eminent — He is all. All prophetic words, all intercession are initiated by His heart's desire, because the prophetic word and the intercession is for the kingdom.

It is written...

> "...hath raised us up together, and made us sit together in heavenly places in Christ Jesus:
>
> "That in the ages to come he might show the exceeding riches of his grace in his kindness toward us through Christ Jesus." Eph. 2:6-7

THE HIDDEN ONES ARE CALLED TO THE
MINISTRY OF INTERCESSION

The one called to be the *Kingdom prophet who is the intercessor* is called to a life behind-the-veil in intercession for the Kingdom. This intense preparation prepares one to live his/her life behind the veil as God's Kingdom prophet. The preparation must be intense and strategic. A strategic part of the preparation will be the stripping away of the trappings that hinder — especially religious trappings.

When one becomes a *Kingdom prophet who is the intercessor*, that one cannot depend on former successes, titles, or knowledge. The King is all, in all, and to all. The one coming into the ministry of the *Kingdom prophet who is the intercessor* is ready and willing to be trained to serve around the throne in intercession first, last, and always.

Since the *Kingdom prophet who is the intercessor* is positioned behind the veil with the King, his/her word is carried out by this *Hidden One* behind the veil in intercession. This *Kingdom prophet intercessor* hidden behind the veil will come to know that the Kingdom prophetic word is given for Kingdom purposes. It is written...

> *"...for there is none other name under heaven given among men, whereby we must be saved."*
> Acts 4:12

Behind the veil, the prophet who is being prepared to become the *Hidden One* in intercession will gain confidence in the power that the intercession wields. The power is in the name of Jesus because the power is in the blood of Jesus. Since true intercession is around the throne, it is orchestrated by the Lord from behind the veil where the *Kingdom prophet who is the intercessor* is the *Hidden One*.

The power the *Kingdom prophet who is the intercessor* wields is a power wrought in the name of Jesus because of the blood Jesus shed on Calvary's Cross. The *Hidden* prophet who is the intercessor enters into the power because of the new and living way which Christ inaugurated through the veil, that is, His flesh.

The *Kingdom prophet who is the intercessor* accesses all the power of Calvary because of having covenant with the King to be His intercessor for this end-time Kingdom prophetic move. In this special ministry of the *Kingdom prophet who is the intercessor* where the *Hidden prophet* serves in prayer around the throne continuously, the *Hidden One's* heart will be enlarged and strengthened to know that his/her intercession establishes the prophetic move of God for God's prophetic people. This one's confidence is enlarged because as that one enters into the call to intercession and accepts the prophetic assignment of intercession to birth in the prophetic word from the heart of the Lord, God hears and answers.

Christ, the High Priest over the Household of God, will bring the *Kingdom prophet who is the intercessor* into a consecrated prayer life as a *Hidden One*. That one will then join in with Jesus who forever lives to make intercession for His prophetic people, for the Kingdom and for the church.

When the *Hidden One* comes into the fullness of the position of *Kingdom prophet who is the intercessor*, he/she will see the King as never seen by that one. That one will have been prepared in intercession to see Him in all His holiness, and all His magnificent splendor, and all His glory.

WHERE TRAINING FOR THE KINGDOM PROPHET BEGINS

The training for the *Kingdom prophet who is the intercessor* begins with one answering the call to be a *Kingdom prophet who is the intercessor*. This then will cause one to become a *Hidden One* for the Lord. Many accept the call to be a prophet, but do not discern that it is also a call to the ministry of intercession. Some accept the call to intercession, but do not discern that etched into that call is the call to be the *Kingdom prophet who is the intercessor*. The truth is that the call to intercession is the call to the prophetic.

What is missing for the many called to intercession is that they have not been trained or prepared to live the *Hidden Life* behind the veil with the King in order to  become the King's Kingdom prophet. The King ministers that truth behind the veil. An intercessor, therefore, must be trained for intercession and for the prophetic behind the veil.

Effective training for the *Kingdom prophet who is the intercessor* does not begin until the one to be trained has entered into covenant with God to assume the position, by saying 'yes' to the ministry of intercession. Although one may have said yes to the prophetic ministry, Kingdom prophets are birthed in Kingdom intercession. This requires a Kingdom covenant where the focus is intercession for the King first, last, and always. When one enters the *covenant to become a Kingdom prophetic intercessor,* that one is prepared then to serve a great God. That is a great calling. It is written...

> *"...Jesus Christ, who is the faithful witness, and the first begotten of the dead, and the prince of the kings of the earth. Unto him that loved us, and washed us from our sins in his own blood,"* Revelation 1:5

The one who answers the call to become a *Kingdom prophet who is the intercessor*, answers the call to become a *Hidden One.* That *one* must then accept the fact that he/she enters into preparation behind the veil in the school in which the King Himself trains the *Kingdom prophet who is the intercessor*. In intercession *the King* teaches all the Kingdom prophet needs to learn in order to have power for the work of the Kingdom.

All the prophet's former victories in prayer mean nothing unless that one enters into the hidden position behind the veil. There, old former understandings give way to truths taught by the King. That is why the prophet who is the intercessor is called to a **Hidden Life** for intercession.

The message is clear. Come to the foot of the cross and prepare to become the **Kingdom prophet who is the intercessor.** This call to hidden position behind the veil is issued especially to the burgeoning prophet to offer him/herself as a learner to be taught of the Lord and to ask the Lord not only to teach him/her prophetic intercession, but also to help him/her be wholehearted. Only the wholehearted can remain Hidden with the King.

Spend one week or more reading and praying the preceding chapter as follows in order to become the *Kingdom prophet who is the intercessor.*

Read a paragraph, then think on the fact of the paragraph, then pray the paragraph asking the Lord about the contents of the paragraph or to make what is written in the paragraph yours. Write what He says to do, and just do it.

Chapter 7

THE *KINGDOM PROPHET* IS A KINGDOM INTERCESSOR

"If ye then be risen with Christ, seek those things which are above, where Christ sitteth on the right hand of God." Colossians 3:1

The *Kingdom prophet who is an intercessor* is called to do everything in the name of the Lord Jesus. That one must keep his/her position seated in heavenly places and must always seek those things above where Christ sits on the right hand of God. That one must forever remember that all authority is...

"...built upon the foundation of the apostles and prophets, Jesus Christ himself being the chief corner stone;" Ephesians 2:20

The *Kingdom prophet who is the intercessor* will come to know that prayers and intercession are effective only on the grounds of death to self. It is written...

"And they that are Christ's have crucified the flesh with the affections and lusts." Galatians 5:24

The *Kingdom prophet who is the intercessor* knows that resurrection is in Jesus Christ only, and he/she needs to die to self to be resurrected in Jesus Christ.

"For if we have been planted together in the likeness of his death, we shall be also in the likeness of his resurrection:

"Knowing this, that our old man is crucified with him, that the body of sin might be destroyed, that henceforth we should not serve sin.

"For he that is dead is freed from sin.

"Now if we be dead with Christ, we believe that we shall also live with him:" Romans 6:5-8

Answering the call to become the *prophet* who is the intercessor is not the conclusion of the matter. It is moving into the full purpose of the calling. The prophet who is the intercessor, therefore, must also pray that the *King* grants him/her the blessed faith and obedience to graduate from the King's school for entrance into the ministry of *Kingdom prophet who is the intercessor.*

Behind the veil is where a change is wrought in the prophet's life by way of intercession. Behind the veil the *prophet* enters into true fellowship with the King and is taught by the Living Lord to take his/her privilege as a Kingdom prophet. That one is called to accept the  assignment to be a *Kingdom prophet who is the intercessor* in God's Kingdom prophetic move-ment for God's prophetic people. Behind the veil, the hidden prophet has learned how prophetic word and prophetic intercession changes, moves, and establishes that which sprang forth from the heart of God.

The Lessons Learned in the Ministry of Intercession

Why the call to the Hidden life? The prophet who is the intercessor learns many lessons while behind the veil with the King. The King teaches the prophet who is the intercessor and the prophet who is the intercessor learns — not as one learns from books, from others, or from the Bible when studying alone.

The prophet who is the intercessor learns of the King and His grace and glory, His will, His ways, His truths, His Holiness. The King teaches the prophet who is the intercessor as that one dwells in the presence of the King behind the veil that the prophet will of necessity pray, intercede, watch, and labor for the prophetic word for the King's prophetic people.

Behind the veil, the hidden prophet who is the intercessor will learn much about the praying, waiting, watching, and co-laboring with the King and about the intercessory prayer of petitioning, and the authoritative prayer of spiritual warfare against satan. The hidden prophet will know and use the authority given for it is written...

"Behold, I give unto you power to tread on serpents and scorpions, and over all the power of the enemy: and nothing shall by any means hurt you."
Luke 10:19

The hidden Kingdom prophet who is the Intercessor is prepared behind the veil to witness the power of Jesus for...

> *"...these signs shall follow them that believe; In my name shall they cast out devils; they shall speak with new tongues."* Mark 16:17

The preparation in intercession for the prophet who is the intercessor to become the Kingdom prophet is intense. That one must become a hidden one in order to know his/her authority. Behind the veil one's faith will become rooted in the King, the Kingdom, and Kingdom prophetic intercession. That one will know that he/she can move mountains. It is written...

> *"...say unto this mountain, ...be thou cast into the sea; and shall not doubt in his heart, but shall believe that those things which he saith shall come to pass; he shall have whatsoever he saith."* Mark 11:23

Behind the veil, the ***Kingdom prophet who is the intercessor*** has been taught the authority given him/her over evil spirits. With prophetic authoritative prayer, the *Hidden* prophet who is the intercessor can command whatever hinders to stop, can bind evil spirits, can lose Holy Spirits and can halt the activities of satan all in the Name of the Lord Jesus. This is the Kingdom prophet who has Kingdom power pouring out from the throne through prophetic intercession.

The Hidden Ones

Many have answered the call to the prophetic, but have not fully accepted the fact that the call is a call to be the *Kingdom prophet who is the intercessor.* Many great church prophets are still prophesying personal prophecy with a smattering of kingdom prophecy interwoven, but do not understand the full ministry of Kingdom prophecy because of having not accepted the call of Kingdom prophetic.

Until the Kingdom prophet accepts the call to be the *Kingdom prophet who is the intercessor*, that one has not accepted the higher purpose of the Kingdom Prophetic Movement. There is an un-tapped power in the prophetic—a power needed to open the way for the King to come in the earth, but that power is brought forth by a *Kingdom prophet who is an intercessor.*

The Kingdom prophet who is called to be the intercessor will come into great power when he/she enters into the secret of God's presence by turning away from all that is of the world. That one will find his/her power by turning away from man and all that is of man, and waiting upon God focusing his/her all on God alone. That one will receive the word of the King. It is written...

> *"...he that loveth me shall be loved of my Father, and I will love him, and will manifest myself to him."*
> John 14:21

Finally, the *Kingdom prophet who is the intercessor* must forsake, give up, and shut out the world, and the life of the world to become Kingdom prophet of the Kingdom prophetic movement of the King. The *Kingdom prophet who is the intercessor* must, therefore, come forth and surrender him/herself to be taught the secrets of the kingdom and to be prepared to dwell in the presence of God forevermore.

Although this book is not written as a "how to" book, it is appropriate to include some practical exercises for the ones called to become the **Kingdom prophet who is the intercessor**. The exercises which include a covenant are included to help one make his/her election sure.

The following covenant agreement and other information are included for that purpose because God does everything by covenant. Although the one reading this book may be established securely in the Covenant of Grace, another covenant becomes necessary for one accepting the call to become a **Kingdom prophet who is the intercessor**.

One may be already in covenant for intercession, for Kingdom intercession—which is a deeper covenant—but this covenant takes one deeper into the Prophetic and into Intercession. The covenant is necessary so that the covenant partner, Jesus Christ, comes alongside to fight the battle for and with His covenant partner. One seeking to become a **Kingdom prophet who is the intercessor** must pause here, read the following covenant prayer, and choose to make his/her election sure by signing the covenant.

Practical Exercise

Acceptance to the call to enter into the ministry of *Kingdom prophet who is the intercessor* in and for the Kingdom of Heaven brings one to the call into Kingdom living. Now is the time to make one's election for the *Kingdom of Heaven* sure and to take the Priestly position of Kingdom prophetic intercessor. Begin first by completing the following Practical Exercise.

This is a serious assignment to help one decide if he/she wants to enter into the Ministry of the *Kingdom prophet who is the intercessor* for the King. The prayers one is called to pray in this position will not be ordinary praying, nor will one be praying when he/she is ready or when he/she feels like it. The one who chooses to enter into this ministry of Kingdom prophetic intercession will spend his/her life praying always around the throne as the Lord leads.

<u>DIRECTIONS:</u> Read the preceding chapter or chapters carefully and slowly. Then go back and reread the paragraph(s). Pray the paragraphs which are relevant to you one several times. Pray in the spirit and ask the Lord to reveal to you the following:

What is the cost of answering the call, and what does the call mean when you answer "yes"?

If you answered "yes" to the above, then continue and complete the following Covenant Agreement prayer.

Covenant Agreement Prayer

Lord, I will to be your **Kingdom prophet who is the intercessor** and am willing to become the **Kingdom prophet who is the Intercessor** for the Kingdom. I cannot become your **Kingdom prophet who is the intercessor** on my own strength, but I can do the following three things and will do them.

I CAN ... choose to say "yes" to the calling.

I CAN ... PRAY; that is, I can keep asking the King for help.

I CAN ... choose to enter into the covenant to become the **Kingdom prophet who is the intercessor** for the King and I believe that I can trust The King to perfect that which concerns me.

Write additional covenants promises in your prayer notebook if necessary.

Name _____
Date:_____

Chapter 8

THE CALL IS PERSONAL...
... WHO WILL ANSWER?

You are being called now to make a decision for this deeper life:

Are you ready for complete, no-compromise surrender?

Are you ready for this?

The Kingdom Prophet called to Strategic Intercession

It is written...

"Then the Lord put forth his hand, and touched my mouth, And the Lord said unto me, Behold, I have put my words in thy mouth.

"See, I have this day set thee over the nations and over the kingdoms, to root out, and to pull down, and to destroy, and to throw down, to build, and to plant."
Jeremiah 1:9-10

Time to Surrender All

This is a call to unconditional surrender of life and everything which pertains to your life. It is the true calling to enter into the fullness of the call to be a Kingdom prophet and to position yourself to be the Vanguard of Kingdom prophet for the King. You are being called now to make a decision for this deeper life.

> **Are you ready for complete, no-compromise surrender? Are you ready for this?**

The scriptures in the Old Testament show that the priesthood is a group of people wholly separated from the world in order to serve God and serve in the presence of the Lord. The call to the **Kingdom prophet who is the intercessor** is a call to a life separated unto the King for Kingdom purposes. When the Lord calls one to *be* Kingdom prophet, it is a call to Kingdom work and Kingdom living.

> **Are you ready for this total commitment?**

Even if prophets believe that their past work and ministry as a prophet have included intercession and that they are anchored securely as God's prophet, the call now is to prepare for the King to establish them in Him. To be established in the King, one must turn away from all that is of the world and of the flesh and seek the King for His will and way in everything that pertains to life and God.

> **Are you ready for this? It is written...**
> *"... many are called, but few are chosen."* **Matthew 22:14**

The call to be God's kingdom prophet is a call to forget everything and everyone, leave everything behind, and find delight in the Lord and Savior, Jesus Christ. He is King of the Kingdom.

> Are you ready for this? It is written...
> *"... many are called, but few are chosen."* Matthew 22:14

It is a decision-making time. From this point, one must go deeper and decide if he/she is willing to go all the way. Here one has come to the point of no return. The time is past for one to glean more information to enjoy or to hope to get help for self. The call is to become the *Kingdom prophet who is the intercessor*. This is a call to sincere prophetic people to come into position with the Lord where the Lord can tell that one what to do and he/she will do it, and then God will do what He and He alone can do.

> Are you ready to choose now this ministry, serving always around the throne of the Lord?

The call to be the *Kingdom prophet who is the intercessor* is a call to come to the King for everything. It begins with intimacy with Jesus Christ as the Kingdom prophet is called to come into a position with God to touch the heart of God, and pray through and work out that which touches the heart of God. The one who chooses to say yes to the call of the *Kingdom prophet who is the intercessor* cannot wander in and out of the Spirit, but must live, move, and walk in the Spirit at all times.

> Are you ready for this total commitment?

Fleshly desires must be nailed to the cross, good and noble deeds must be put to rest, and religious activities must be sanctified and made spiritual. Many will need to be stopped, and some will be modified. This is not a call to the ministry only or to church work. This is about a life totally given over to the King for His use.

Are You Ready for This Total Commitment?

Too few of God's children choose to pay the price for this coveted position to become a *Kingdom prophet who is the intercessor*. Too many spend their Christian life wandering around partially or fully blinded to God and His magnificent glory because they have not come close enough to touch or experience Him. The called-out *Kingdom prophet who is the intercessor* will experience and touch God.

Are You Ready for This Total Commitment?

The call to be a *Kingdom prophet who is the intercessor* is a special call. It is the highest calling in the Kingdom of Heaven, and many miss this wonderful privilege because they are not willing to pay the price, and/or they are not sure of the call, and/or because they are not ready to pay the price to enter this calling.

Are You Ready to Give Up Everything for this Call — Fame, Recognition, A MINISTRY, Everything?

Greater is the call to be a *Kingdom prophet who is the intercessor*, than any other call upon one's life, because God the Father has called as many as will for this great calling to fulfill a special work He has in His heart.

This is a great blessing for the one who answers this call, but one must choose because once the choice is made, that one cannot choose to return to a slippery Christian walk. Are you willing to pray here and ask God to show you your former slippery Christian walk? When He reveals your slippery Christian walk, are you willing to list what He says, and choose to give up one thing at a time, one by one?

The call to be a Kingdom prophet who is the intercessor is a spiritual calling; and one must enter into it in the Spirit, by the Spirit and through the Spirit. It is too gigantic a call to enter in by one's own strength — one must depend on God totally. That means total unconditional commitment to God and deep cleansing, deep healing, and great deliverance for the one called.

"... many are called, but few are chosen." Matthew 22:14

Many who have been called to be prophets of the Church and in the Church are the ones now called to be the Kingdom *Intercession*, but few are chosen to be the **Kingdom prophet who is the intercessor.** This is a very serious call, and carries a heavy requirement. Before one says 'yes' to this calling, one will surely need to count the cost. The Kingdom prophetic intercessor gives up every aspect of life for this call, just as Jesus Christ, the High Priest, gave His life for the believer's salvation.

Are You Ready for This Total Commitment?

The cost of the ministry of Kingdom prophetic intercession is death to self and every desire for self. It requires death to life as one knows it and death to one's desires, ambitions, hopes, dreams. **The Kingdom prophet** *who is the intercessor* enters directly into the presence of the Lord as he/she serves around the throne in the presence of the Lord.

> Are you ready to give up everything for this call—fame, recognition, A MINISTRY—Everything?

The call to be a *Kingdom prophet who is the intercessor* in the Kingdom of Heaven is a call to be separated unto the Lord and dedicated to His service. It means that one is in the world but not of the world. It means that all one does is done unto the Lord and that one has his/her being in Jesus Christ. It means that one is taught of the Lord and that one is for the Lord in all things.

> It's time to make that decision here now, never to take it back – Are you ready?

The *Kingdom prophet who is the intercessor* will pay the same price to be a *Kingdom prophet who is the intercessor* that Jesus Christ paid for mankind. The Father had to send His only Son, and the blood that the Son shed was needed to save the whole world. The life that one gives up will be for the Kingdom of Heaven. It will put that one out front in the End-time Battle of the Kingdom of Heaven.

> Are you ready to pay the price? Are you ready for this total commitment?

The conditions of one's life and things happening around one, and the distance some who are called to be prophets are from the Lord, require more than prayers that may or may not reach heaven. It requires a life given over so completely to the King that nothing else matters. The call is to be a *Kingdom prophet who is the intercessor* in the Kingdom of Heaven.

> **Are you ready for this mighty call, and the price you will have to pay for Kingdom prophetic intercession?**

It is time now to make the once-for-all-time commitment to take your position as a *Kingdom prophet who is the intercessor* and become a Kingdom prophet. That can only be done when one gives his/her life to the ministry of the *Kingdom prophet who is the intercessor.*

> *Are you ready to make that decision here, now, never to take it back? — Are you ready?*

The one called to be the **Kingdom prophet who is the intercessor** must decide if his/her lifestyle and life's work require too much of one's time to make this type of commitment. One must choose to make a commitment and pay the price to be the Kingdom prophet. The call to be the *Kingdom prophet who is the intercessor* is not only to pray, but also to come in position with the King so that He can tell His prophet what to do, and that one will do it. Then the King will do what He and He alone can do.

> It is time to make that decision here now, never to take it back. Are you ready?

The one who says 'yes' to this call to be the Kingdom prophet for the Kingdom of Heaven must know the requirements and be willing to meet the requirements. This call will of necessity require searching one's own heart and examining one's own life, one's ways, and one's behavior. It is going to require a holy, committed life.

> **Are you ready for this deep spiritual walk and deep spiritual life?**

Because this is such a special call and the promise is to the Kingdom prophet if he/she will rise to the call, that one needs to make a formal commitment to the Lord and enter into a covenant agreement with God and, if possible, others to continue to the end.

> *It is time to make that decision here now, never to take it back. Are you ready?*

This is a call that will not make you popular or help you gain favor in the ministry. Instead, it will call one to give up ministries and much activity in the religious arena in order to spend more time with the Master in intercession.

> **Time to make that decision here now, never to take it back. Are you ready?**

DECISION-MAKING TIME
For Accepting the Kingdom Call of the Hour

It is a decision-making time. From this point, one must go deeper, and choose if he/she is willing to go all the way. We have come to the point of no return.

The time is past for one to glean more information to enjoy or to hope to get help for self. The time is now for total, unconditional surrender.

Spend a week praying and/or writing your covenant of intercession. If you want to sign the covenant below, read it and pray. Pray it each time you meet with the Lord. If you want to write your own, sign it, and have it witnessed by someone in spiritual authority.

If you want to use the Covenant which follows, read and reread the covenant below and sign it as your FINAL COVENANT FOR ACCEPTANCE OF THIS SPECIAL KINGDOM CALL.

COVENANT FOR THE
Kingdom prophet who is the intercessor

Lord, I, covenant with you this day (yr.) to enter into the call into greater service--the call to the New Beginning of Kingdom Intercession. I hereby answer the call to intercession.

*I choose to begin whatever is necessary to become the **Kingdom prophet who is the intercessor** for the King. I promise to prepare to become a **Kingdom prophet who is the intercessor**.*

I accept the call to let the King be everything in my life. I abandon myself to the King. I accept the call to be a **Kingdom prophet who is the intercessor.**

I commit myself today, my Lord and Master, to take my position with Christ as a **Kingdom prophet who is the intercessor.** I promise not to strain nor strive. I will cast myself on the King and know that then and only then will I have the full power of the Spirit operating within me.

I will press on toward the fullness of the call to be a **Kingdom prophet who is the intercessor** with the King. I will forsake family and other loved ones if called by you to do so. I will love The Lord more than myself.

Dear Lord, I promise to come to the King regularly to sup with Him, to sit in His presence, to learn from the King, and to spend consecrated time with The King. I will not boast in self, in anyon,e or anything except Jesus Christ.

I will not count myself more than Jesus. I will remember that The King is the source of everything -- that He is first and will always be first in my life. I will have no other god before the King. I will praise the King, worship, love, honor, obey, thank, and trust Him.

Signed _____   Date _____

The covenant prayer prayed on the previous page is for the life of a Kingdom Prophet Who is the Intercessor...

Kingdom prophets who are intercessors are positioned to serve the King and live a life unto the Lord. The scriptures reveal that Kingdom prophets lived their lives separated unto the Lord, and they loved and obeyed God's Word.

Kingdom prophets lived a life of obedience to the King, i.e. Ezekiel, Jeremiah, Isaiah, etc. They offered burnt offerings, making intercession for the people, serving as a prophet to the people and as a Kingdom Intercessor for the Kingdom of Heaven.

The Kingdom prophet will stand before the Lord in intercession, warring, and serving as a watchman.

THE *KINGDOM PROPHET WHO IS THE INTERCESSOR* CALLED...

NOTES

BOOKS BY

PERNELL H. HEWING, Ph.D., Th.D.

INTERCESSION
Calling Forth the Bride of Christ for Intercession
A treatise on the Calling, the Stripping, the Clothing, the Adorning, and the Warfare of the Bride of Christ. This book issues a call to the reader to come into the high place of honor the Lord wills for every born-again believer-- the bridal chamber of the Lord. The book presents practical exercises which leads one along the pathway to intimacy with the Lord which only the bride of Christ in intercession attains.

The Royal Priesthood, Made According to God's Plan
An Intercessory Prayer and Word Training Manual designed to lead one into deeper depths of Prayer and to prepare Intercessors, Prayer Group Leaders, and Ministers for greater Kingdom work. (CDs Available)

The Inner Court Ministry with Christ,
The Master/Teacher in the School of Prayer
This book calls every believer to the Inner Life, a Hidden Life, spent dwelling in the presence of the Lord with Christ in the School of Prayer. The Ministry of the Inner Court prepares one for powerful kingdom work undergirded with powerful, priestly prayer. The book leads one into consecrated prayer for healing of the soul, the mind, heart and the Spirit.

The Call to Adonai, Your Lord and Master And to the Bondslave Experience

This book leads a believer to lay his/her life on the altar and take up the mantle of intercession. It leads one to a complete surrender, then to birth in his/her ministry, and onto a life of continuous abiding before the Lord so that all the intercessor does is ordered by the Lord.

The Ministry of the Mizpeh Covenant

This book focuses on the truth of the meaning of covenant-making and preparing for battle. It calls one to give up idols one must deal with. It then presents the truth of covenant-making from salvation to the covenant of grace to the purpose of covenant-making. A special feature of this book is an Introduction to the cross life.

The New Sound of Zion

This is a photogenic view of End-Time Zion where the Lion of Judah resides. This book issues a call to every born-again believer in Jesus Christ to prepare for a new sound from heaven to open the way for the Lion of Judah to come. The New sound of Zion is a call to worshipers, dancers, musicians, and intercessors to choose to pay the price to release the New Sound whether it be song, dance, music or Intercession to open the way for the Lion of Judah to roar in the Church.

The Hebron Ministry...
A Ministry of Faith, Rest, and Refuge

This book leads one to and gives meaning to going wholehearted with God. The End-Time Believer enters into Faith and REST as God ordains. When one goes wholehearted with God, the Believer will find refuge with Him.

El Shaddai

The believer who enters into this ministry will receive new life, revival, restoration and "The Blessing". The believer will understand how much he/she is in need of a blessing, if that one missed out on the "Family Blessing" during childhood. This book also leads to the healing of the wounded spirit, awakening of the sleeping spirit, and release of the imprisoned spirit.

HEALING

The Healing Streams of Bethesda

This a call to a place of healing--a place to enter into the waters of life. The message of this book points one to the healer, Jesus Christ. A special focus is placed on the three keys of healing: the grace of faith, the grace of hope, and the grace of love.

Come to Gilgal for Circumcision of the Heart
This book is the treatise of the message in Joshua 1-6 relating it to the need for circumcision of the heart for a deeper walk with God. It deals with putting an end to wilderness wandering after salvation.. (CDs Available)

The Ministry of Jehovah Rapha with Concepts of Divine Healing
In Rapha one finds healing for deep wounds, emotional scars, debilitating illness and other traumas for which many have given up hope. The Lord comes unto us in Rapha to heal not only the body, but also heals the soul and spirit.

MINISTRY

Getting to Know the Holy Spirit and Preparing for Holy Ghost Baptism with Fire
This book is written for the purposes of pleading with the believer to seek for all what was promised and to be satisfied with nothing less than full power from on high. A special focus of this book is Baptism with Holy Ghost Pentecostal fire and preparation to work the works of God in power.

Practical Aspects of the Body of Christ and the Five-Fold Ministries for the Kingdom
A deep study of the Body of Christ and Five-Fold Ministry and the various aspects of the ministry with attention being given to the call and qualifications.

The End-Time Call for Spiritual Mentoring, Teaching, Training, Fathering, Mothering, to Apostolic Covering

This book explains the different assignments God gives His servants for another's life i.e. mentoring, teaching, training, spiritual parenting (which sometimes includes natural reparenting) to Apostolic covering. Also included is special information on armour bearing.

Shiloh El-Beth-el, Calling Believers in Christ...
...in Preparation for the Ministry of the Kingdom of Heaven

Shiloh El-Beth-el is representative of the Kingdom of Heaven – the Kingdom of God on earth. It brings into focus God's ways of dealing with mankind and how it establishes His plan and purpose for and with mankind. It takes one back to the first church in the wilderness and to the Levitical Ministry of the Old Testament.

Shammah, the Ministry of the Prophet/Intercessor and of God's Prophetic People

This is a book to help the believer understand the office of the prophet/prophetess, prophecy, and this end-time prophetic movement. The messages also focus on the life and calling of the Prophet Intercessor.

MINISTRY INTERCESSION

Spiritual Authority: Understanding and Submitting to Spiritual Authority Brings Power, Authority, and Anointing

This book presents a microscopic view of Spiritual Authority in and for the Ministry and the facets of Spiritual Authority often overlooked or not known by those who *"... walked not after the flesh but after the spirit."* **Romans 8:4b.** This book helps one to understand how to enter into and walk in the authority of the believer and how to receive and walk in the anointing.

Repentance and Remission for Entrance into Kingdom Apostolic Work

This is a book of practical exercises to prepare one for the ultimate Kingdom ministry of remitting sins. The Purpose is to take the reader on a journey of forgiveness, Holy Ghost repentance, and remission of sins for oneself. It is at the end of the journey that one is prepared for Kingdom ministry.

DELIVERANCE

Smashing the Influence of Tap-Root Bondages

This book focuses on smashing the influence of the tap-root bondages of pride, rejection, rebellion, stubbornness, disobedience, and fear. It is designed to prepare one for intercession by leading one into deeper revelations of these areas in their own lives.

The Call to the Ministry of Deliverer Jesus Christ Jehovah-Sabaoth

The purpose of this book is to issue a call to the "called out" people of God to look together into the Word of God to find answers. The ministry of Sabaoth is for those who have come to the end of their strength and need deliverance—Jehovah-Sabaoth meets failure and offers deliverance.

PERSONAL GROWTH

In the Garden with the Risen Savior

This book is for anyone seeking a life centered in Christ or already anchored in Christ. It reveals how close God can be to His own whether one trusts Him completely or whether one accepts His love, His kindness, His forgiveness.

Bring your Life to Divine Order Through Two Forty-Day Consecrations

Presenting consecrations of fasting, travailing prayer, physical cleansing, and spiritual cleansing in preparation for unconditional surrender. This book presents guidelines for two 40-day consecrations for unconditional surrender. The first is a consecration of fasting, travailing prayer, cleaning, and putting the physical environment in order. The second is a consecration in prayer and the Word of God which leads to spiritual cleansing.

Into the Depths with Jesus

The writer captures the heart of God as she records His messages for the work of the Kingdom. An account of one person's journey with God, this book speaks to all who are seeking a deeper walk with God.

The Threefold Calvary Experiences of a Christian: New Life, Death, and Resurrection in Christ.

This book is a call to look to Calvary for New Life in Jesus Christ. The information leads one through a Gethsemane Experience to death to self and into a Bond-slave Relationship with Jesus.

The Book of Ephesians

To get the Word of God in your heart, begin with the book of Ephesians. These are the study and ministry CDs and aid for memorizing scriptures. (CD only)

From Spiritual/Financial Insolvency to Financial/Spiritual Abundance

This is not a "how-to" book to read to glean more information about finances. It is a book to change your position in Christ. This can only happen as one completes Practical Exercises as directed.

FAMILY INTERCESSION

Calling Forth the Family (Priest) Intercessor
To Destroy Generational Line Curses

Guidelines for entering into a life of intercession and work of Intercession for the family. Information in this book introduces the call to be **the Family (Priest) Intercessor** and what it takes to break the back of Satan and take family members out of his hands.

Understanding and Destroying the Power in Generational Line Curses

This book is written is such a manner that one could learn enough to enter into the call to become **the Family (Priest) Intercessor.** As you grasp the information given here and say **'yes'** to what the Lord is saying, you will enter into a depth with Jesus where Satan will not be able to touch.

Divine Exchange of Curses for Blessings

This book gives an account of the battle to release the blessings in the family bloodline. It is the opposite of breaking curses, but the battle is just as fierce for unlocking blessings in the family bloodline.

Spiritual Journey into Intercession for Families in Desperate Situations

This book provides practical guidelines for interceding for a family member or for families in desperate situations. This book also calls the one praying into the position of Family (**Priest**) Intercessor.

Restoring the Beauty of Holy Matrimony

A manual of information for Married Couples, Couples Planning Marriage, Couples Planning Reconciliation after a period of Separation, and Couples contemplating divorce, or Couples locked into a troubled marriage, and for pastors, ministers and other marriage counselors.

THE TRIBES OF ISRAEL

The Tribe of Judah

This book provides a panoramic view of the Tribe of Judah beginning with his birth in Genesis and continues on into Revelations where the Lion as the Tribe of Judah comes on the scene. This gives a detailed account of Judah's ministry as worshiper, warrior, intercessor, king and priest.

The Tribe of Simeon

This book provides an all encompassing view of the Tribe of Simeon commencing with his birth in Genesis and culminating in Revelations. This book gives a detailed account of Simeon's ministry as the Sword of the Lord in the End-time Church.

The Tribe of Benjamin

This book provides an all encompassing view of the Tribe of Benjamin commencing with his birth in Genesis and culminating in Revelations. This book gives a detailed account of the ministry of the End-Time Benjamites who come to the End-Time church preaching the Gospel with power.

The Tribe of Asher

This book provides an all microscopic review of the Tribe of Asher as presented in the Old Testament, and introduces the ministry of the End-time Tribe of the Asherite in the Body of Christ as the one who has died to every desire except to engage in the ministry of Prayer, Intercession and warfare. The one who has the End-time ministry of Asher chooses to spend his/her life around the throne in the bridal chamber to receive the heart of the King for the Kingdom.

The Tribe of Manasseh

Manasseh is the son of Joseph adopted by Jacob as one of his own sons. The ministry of Manasseh is the key for the Kingdom as this is the ministry which will lift the church above the healing and wholeness to healing for the nations.

The Tribe of Ephraim

Ephraim is the second son of Joseph who was adopted by Jacob as one of his own. He is the one over which Jacob crossed his hand and gave him firstborn blessings although he was the second born. This book introduces the ministry of Ephraim for the Kingdom which is the one given to healing for the backsliding church.

The Tribe of Gad

The ministry of the End-time Tribe of Gad is deliverance of the church out of the hand of the enemy so that the church will be prepared for the Kingdom. This book provides the revelation that the higher purpose of the End-time Gadite ministry is to go beyond opening prison doors of the believers in Jesus Christ who are in need of deliverance, but also to deliver the church from the throes of satan and from satan's demonic infiltration.

The Tribe of Issachar

This book introduces Issachar as the Burden-bearer for the church. The End-Time Issacharite not only knows the times and seasons, but carries a ministry in for the Kingdom which encompasses one or all of the following: Intercessor, prophet, prophet intercessor, spiritual father, pastor, prayer warrior.

The Tribe of Zebulun

This book gives a historical account of the life and works of the Tribe of Zebulun in Israel and into the ministry for the Kingdom. The ministry of the End-Time Zebulunites is a Kingdom Evangelistic ministry.

The Tribe of Dan

The ministry of the Danite in the Kingdom is multifaceted, but it begins and ends with a ministry of judgment. The Danite ministry will open the way for healing of the believer which is needed because of one missing the blessing of natural parents. The End-time Danite will be positioned in the church and the Kingdom to know and to see—Especially see and discern an unholy priest/pastor/leader in the Church

The Tribe Napthtali

The Ministry of the End-Time Napthali is Prophetic Intercessor, Watchman and warrior. Napthtali is a hind let loose: he giveth goodly words. The Ministry of the Naphtali in the Kingdom is the Prophet-Intercessor in the Kingdom who has been brought into a hidden place with the Lord in order to be the hind loosed to destroy the enemy camp in and over the church.

The Tribe of Reuben

Reuben is the first son of Jacob, but did not receive his firstborn birthright. The ministry of the End-Time Reubenite is to bring the church to see the Son, Jesus Christ. As the Reubenites come on the scene in the church, eyes will be opened to see the Son, high and lifted up, calling the church up higher to enter into the Kingdom.

The Tribe of Levi

This book will lead the reader along a pathway to unconditional surrender and to live as the priest of old in order to become End-Time ministers of the Kingdom. The ministry of the End-Time Levite is the ministry of the Royal Priesthood. The signs of the times are upon the Church for the End-Time Levitical Minstry to come forth and open the way for the King to come.

Order from:
Sanctuary Word Press,
921 W. Main St., Whitewater, WI 53190-1706
Phone: (262) 473-7472 † Fax: (262) 473-9724
E-mail: hewingph@idcnet.com
Website: www.thesanctuarywhitewater.com

THE MINISTRY OF THE PROPHETIC INTERCESSOR

PERNELL H. HEWING, PH.D., TH.D.

www.ingramcontent.com/pod-product-compliance
Lightning Source LLC
Chambersburg PA
CBHW051456290426
44109CB00016B/1780